Beneath the Ice

Contents

Martyn Beardsley
Character illustrations by Jon Stuart

Searching the hidden depths

In August, 2008, the Canadian icebreaker ship the *Sir Wilfrid Laurier* nudged through the ice off Canada's north coast. Scientists left the ship and braved the sub-zero temperature to explore. They found some old nails and bits of copper sheeting. To the scientists, these things were as exciting as treasure.

The researchers returned to the icebreaker and began to sweep the seas around the island using hi-tech **sonar** equipment.

This is the *Louis S. St-Laurent*—a modern icebreaker that belongs to the Canadian Coast Guard.

Arctic Circle

Greenland

Alaska

Canada

United States

They were looking for evidence of two ships and the men who sailed in them.

The two ships they were searching for were called the *Erebus* and *Terror*. Over 150 years ago, they were trapped and crushed by the ice. It is thought that the ships sank to the bottom of the ocean as the ice retreated. The frozen Arctic, however, was not ready to give up its secrets just yet.

The whereabouts of the ships remain a mystery. Who was leading the ships? Where they were going? Why did 129 men willingly go into this harsh and unforgiving icy region? In this book we look at some of the answers.

View from the deck of a modern icebreaker

How did they get through all that ice?

Let's go exploring!

On May 19, 1845, two small, sturdy ships, the *Erebus* and *Terror*, left behind cheering crowds lining the River Thames and sailed out into the open sea. They were heading north in search of the Northwest Passage. The expedition leader was Sir John Franklin. His wife Jane and daughter Eleanor were among those watching the ships depart. He waved in their direction, but they were so far away he couldn't be sure that they had seen him. It was the last time he would ever see them.

What is the Northwest Passage?

The Northwest Passage is a sea route through the Arctic Ocean, along the northern coast of North America. It connects the Atlantic and Pacific Oceans.

In the 1800s, voyages to places like China and India for silk and spices to sell in Europe involved long journeys south. Boats had to sail around Africa or South America. People wanted to find a way through the icy seas to the north because the trip would be quicker, cheaper, and as much as 5,000 miles shorter. However, the seas were dangerous and frozen solid for much of the year.

It wasn't only about trade. The first explorer to prove the Northwest Passage existed would win fame and perhaps even fortune, so many people tried.

Arctic facts

- A large part of the Arctic is covered in permanent ice.
- The ground is mostly permafrost—ground at, or below, freezing point for two or more years.
- Icebergs are found in the Arctic. They are massive pieces of frozen, fresh water that break off from a glacier or ice sheet.
- In Northern Territories, the Arctic winter is 9 months long, during which time the "night" lasts 20–24 hours.
- In winter, temperatures drop to nearly –60°F.
- July and August are the only months when snow doesn't cover the ground.

This map shows the Northwest Passage (marked in red). As you can see, there are a few different routes!

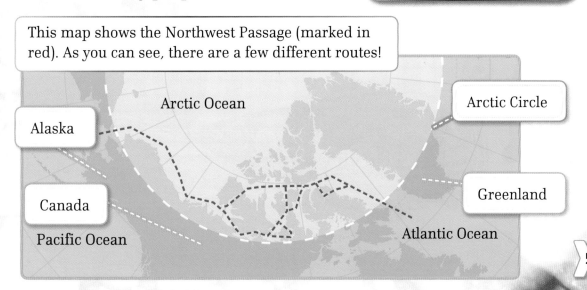

Arctic Ocean

Arctic Circle

Alaska

Canada

Greenland

Pacific Ocean

Atlantic Ocean

Those who tried and failed

The Vikings

Some believe that the Vikings were the first people to try to find a passage through the ice-bound islands off the coast of Canada.

Who were they? People from Scandinavia who ventured throughout Europe as raiders and traders

When did they live? Between AD 750 and AD 1050

What is the evidence to show that they tried to sail the Northwest Passage? One place Vikings settled was Greenland, which lies near the starting point for Northwest Passage journeys (see page 5).

There was a period of warmer temperatures at this time that may have made traveling by boat easier. Iron boat rivets and a piece of cloth, like that used in Viking clothing, have been found in the area.

Imagine being the first person to discover a new land.

Sir Francis Drake

Who was he? An English sailor and explorer

When did he live? 1540–1596

Why did he try to sail the Northwest Passage? Drake was the first captain to **circumnavigate** the globe. In 1579, he sailed up the west coast of America attacking England's enemy, the Spanish. Then he tried to sail farther north and return to Britain through the Passage.

How far did he get? It is believed that he reached at least as far north as Alaska before the freezing conditions drove him back south.

The ship Francis Drake used to circumnavigate the world was called the *Golden Hind*.

Captain Cook

Alaska 1778
Capt.ⁿ *JAMES COOK*

The farthest point north that Cook reached was Alaska.

Who was he? One of the world's greatest explorers

When did he live? 1728–1779

What happened? Captain James Cook was not the first man to discover Australia and New Zealand. He was, however, the first to make proper records of their locations and bring them to the attention of the world. During his voyages, he circumnavigated the world twice and made charts of the oceans and islands which are still used today. However, even he was defeated by the ice of the Northwest Passage.

Sir John Franklin was born seven years after Captain Cook died. By this time, many people believed that the Northwest Passage was too difficult and dangerous to sail through. However, people still wanted to know for sure.

Who was Sir John Franklin?

Sir John Franklin was a sailor and explorer. He wanted to be the first to conquer the Northwest Passage. He was chosen by the British Royal Navy to lead the 1845 expedition to the Passage because he had already done a great deal of exploring in the Arctic region by ship and on land. Read on to find out about his missions to the Arctic region.

Sir John Franklin timeline

1786
Born Lincolnshire, England

1800
Joined the British Royal Navy

1803
Shipwrecked while exploring Australia

1805
Took part in the Battle of Trafalgar. Noise from the cannon fire left him deaf in one ear.

MISSION 3
1825
Second overland expedition to Canada

1829
Knighted

1836
Became lieutenant-governor of Tasmania, Australia

1844
Returned to England

MISSION 4
1845
Northwest Passage expedition

Franklin's mission files

MISSION ONE—THE NORTH POLE

His first mission, in 1818, was part of an attempt by two ships to sail to the **North Pole**. Both ships were almost trapped and crushed by the icy seas. The crews could feel their wooden ships being pushed up into the air. They could hear the wood creaking and splitting as the water froze up around them without warning. The battered, leaky ships made it back to Britain six months later.

The *Trent* trapped in ice.

What do you think Franklin must have been like?

1808
Promoted to lieutenant

1815
Wounded during British war with America

MISSION 1
1818
Commanded HMS *Trent* in North Pole expedition

MISSION 2
1819
First overland expedition to Canada. Promoted to commander

1822
Promoted to captain

1847
Died

1850
Traces of Franklin's expedition found

1859
Message in **cairn** found telling of Franklin's death

MISSION TWO—NORTHERN CANADA

In 1819, Franklin led an overland expedition to northern Canada. He wanted to explore the coast to see whether ships attempting the Northwest Passage might be able to get through. The expedition was a disaster. Franklin and his men experienced some of the coldest conditions ever known.

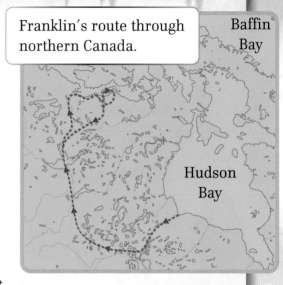

Franklin's route through northern Canada.

Baffin Bay

Hudson Bay

Franklin later said that the return journey was one of the worst experiences of his life. Food ran out, and the starving party could only make painfully slow progress through the deep snow and blasting winds. The temperature dipped as low as −42°F. Eventually the only food they had was a **moss** which tasted so foul and bitter that it made some men sick. Franklin left the weakest men behind while he and the rest carried on. When they reached a log cabin where he had arranged for emergency food supplies to be left, they found the place bare.

Franklin wrote:

> "The whole of our party shed tears, not so much for our own fate, as for that of our friends in the rear, whose lives depended entirely on our sending immediately relief from this place."

Franklin and his men were almost living skeletons by now. There was no food. They ate rotten bones, old deer skins, which they had to fry to make chewable, and even their own leather **moccasins**. (Franklin is still known as "the man who ate his boots.")

He recorded:

> "We perceived our strength decline every day . . . when we were once seated, the greatest effort was necessary in order to rise, and we frequently had to lift each other from our seats."

He must have been desperate to eat his boots!

Much earlier, Franklin had sent one of his men off to seek help. Finally the man arrived with help and food. Eleven out of the twenty men had died. Franklin had travelled nearly 5,550 miles on foot and by canoe. He discovered areas which had previously been blank on European maps.

Braving the cold

The Arctic region is one of the coldest areas in the world. The lowest recorded temperature in the area is –62°F. In these conditions, the moisture from your breath freezes in the air. One of Franklin's men who went out hunting was so covered in ice when he returned that no one recognized him!

How cold is the Arctic?

Average lowest temperature (Fahrenheit)		
	Arctic Bay, Canada	New York, NY
January	-27	27
February	-33	29
March	-26	35
April	-15	45
May	12	54
June	30	64
July	36	69
August	36	68
September	27	61
October	10	50
November	-9	42
December	-22	32

Arctic survival tips

- Eat lots! The average adult male needs roughly 2,000 calories a day. On an Arctic expedition, a man consuming 6,000 calories a day—three times the normal amount—might still expect to lose weight!

- Don't underestimate the time it takes to do things in icy weather. Always allow plenty of time to make a shelter.

- Keep dry. Keep warm. Wear many layers of clothing to protect yourself against the freezing temperatures (see opposite).

- If you need to cross thin ice, spread your weight evenly over the ice by lying down and crawling over it.

- To walk over deep snow, make a pair of snowshoes by using strips of leather, cloth, or other suitable material (or take some snow shoes with you!). These will keep you from completely sinking into the snow.

Traditional and modern snowshoes

Franklin's second attempt

MISSION THREE—NORTHERN CANADA

Even while he was recovering from his 1819 expedition, Franklin was planning a second expedition to the same region to complete the mapping of the coast. In 1825, he led the second expedition to northern Canada. Learning from the harsh lessons of the first trip, he made sure everything was perfectly organized. This time, no lives were lost. The closest anyone came to death was a sailor who decided to go sliding down a very steep, snow-covered hill on his bottom and shredded his pants to pieces!

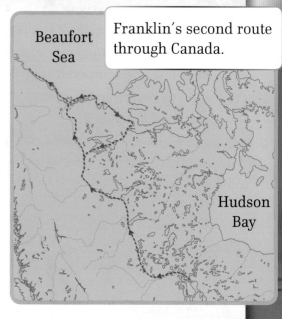

Beaufort Sea

Franklin's second route through Canada.

Hudson Bay

What did Franklin eat?

- Franklin and his team could carry some food supplies, but they also had to hunt animals to eat, such as deer, bears, and fish.

- Before the food ran out, Franklin's men ate *pemmican*: meat mixed with fat and dried out over a fire or in the sun to make it last longer.

How to make pemmican

You will need:

- 1 cup of dried meat (deer, moose, caribou, or beef)
- 1 cup of dried fruit or berries (currants, raisins, blueberries, apricots, or cherries)
- 1 cup of melted butter
- A little salt

1. Crush the dried meat into a powder.
2. Grind one or two different dried fruits or berries.
3. Mix the dried meat powder with the dried fruit powder. Add a little salt to add flavor.
4. Pour the butter over the mixture and stir until the mixture sticks together.
5. Spread it out like a dough and allow it to cool.
6. When cool, cut into small pieces and store in an airtight container.

Mmm . . . not bad.

I wouldn't like to eat it every day, though!

Franklin had traveled a similar distance as the first expedition and mapped 1,200 miles of the coastline. What he saw was enough to convince him that sailing through the Northwest Passage might just be possible—and he wanted to be the man to do it.

Into the unknown

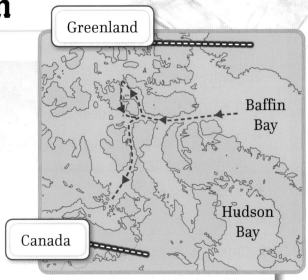

Greenland

Baffin Bay

Canada

Hudson Bay

MISSION FOUR—THE NORTHWEST PASSAGE

Franklin's 1845 mission was to be the best prepared and most hi-tech there had ever been. The ships he took—the *Erebus* and *Terror*—were specially strengthened. They also were equipped with what were then two new aids. One was propellers. As well as helping to move the ship when there was no wind, the steam engines which powered them helped to heat the ship. Coal to fuel the engines was limited however, so the propellers couldn't be used often. The other new aid was canned food. This was a recent invention, which meant that food could last longer. The supplies loaded into the ships were calculated to be able to last for three years. Franklin and his crew expected to be stuck in the ice for long periods.

Sailors wrote their last letters home early on in the mission. Franklin told his wife he was thinking of her and all his family and friends:

"Oh, how I wish I could write to each of them to assure them of the happiness I feel in my officers, my crew, and my ship."

One of Franklin's officers wrote of how their commander told them tales of his previous expeditions. Everyone was very fond of Franklin. The officer wrote:

"He is full of life and energy . . . and of all men he is the most fitted for the command of an enterprise requiring sound sense and great perseverance."

Another officer warned his wife that he might be away for quite some time:

". . . do not allow any person to dishearten you on the length of our absence, but look forward to the hope that **providence** will at length of time restore us safely to you."

Two months later an English whaling ship came upon the *Erebus* and *Terror* in **Baffin Bay**. The captain of the whaling ship was invited on board Franklin's ship and found everyone in good spirits for the adventure ahead. He was the last British man to see any of the crew alive.

The search for Franklin

At first, no one was too surprised that there was no news from the expedition. When nothing had been heard from Franklin after two years, though, people began to worry, and plans were made for rescue missions. Between 1848 and 1859, up to 40 ships were sent to look for survivors or traces of Franklin's expedition within the icy depths.

RESCUE FILE

Led by: Sir John Richardson,
Sir James Clarke Ross,
Captain Henry Kellet, and
Dr. Jon Rae

Year: 1848

The Arctic council discussing plans to rescue Franklin and his men.

In 1848, an expedition of explorers attempted to find Franklin. Sir John Richardson was Franklin's best friend. He had accompanied Franklin on the overland expeditions of 1819 and 1825. Richardson returned to the region that had almost cost him his life and attempted a search from the coast.

Another friend and fellow explorer, Sir James Clarke Ross, attempted to follow Franklin's route. A third explorer, Captain Henry Kellet, entered the Northwest Passage from the opposite direction. Ross's ships became trapped in drifting ice that carried them back many miles the way they had come, causing them to give up and return to England.

In 1854, the explorer Dr. John Rae was still leading the search for Franklin by land. He sent back stories of **Inuit** who had seen parties of starving white men and who had items traded from them, including watches, telescopes, and a silver plate with Sir John Franklin's name inscribed on it.

Inuit people still live in the Arctic region today.

Dr. Rae was searching for 6 years! I wonder where Franklin could have gone?

RESCUE FILE

Led by: Captain Horatio Austin

Year: 1850

The ships used in the 1848 search were sent out again. In 1850, evidence of Franklin's expedition was found: pieces of clothing, timber from ships or boats, tin cans, and other items. The graves of three sailors were also found. The graves were marked with wooden "gravestones," which gave the names, ages, and dates of death of the three men.

Despite these discoveries, Captain Austin got into trouble for bringing his ships home earlier than he was supposed to. The navy, which had paid for the trip, thought he should have expanded his search in the place where his team had found the graves.

One of Franklin's relics that Captain Austin brought back from his rescue expedition was a clay pipe.

The site of the three graves found by Captain Austin.

RESCUE FILE

Led by: Sir Francis Leopold McClintock

Year: 1857

These snow goggles were found abandoned.

Sir John Franklin's second wife, Jane, sent out the ship, the *Fox*, paid for using her own money. This search, led by Francis McClintock, found more belongings from Franklin's expedition. He spoke to Inuit and heard more stories of dying white men. In 1859, searchers on the *Fox* were still in the region. They found the only written record left by officers of the *Erebus* and *Terror*, confirming the death of Sir John Franklin and others.

This is an artist's impression of the *Fox* from 1859.

The search for Franklin amid the hidden depths of the Northwest Passage attracted much public interest. As rescue and recovery missions failed, people began to write to the newspapers suggesting ways to find Franklin.

An engineer called Shepherd wanted to blow holes in the ice using explosives.

October 6th, 1849

Dear Editor:

I would like to propose a simple solution to allow Franklin rescue missions to forge a clear and easy path through the icy waters of the Northwest Passage. I have recently returned from the Danube, where parts of the river had layers of ice four feet in thickness due to weeks of sub-zero temperatures. To create "roads" in the water, a shell of gunpowder was exploded and large masses of ice flew in all directions. It allowed navigation to occur in the space that the explosion had left. I believe that gunpowder is the answer, and I will obligingly, for a fee, come along and prepare the gunpowder on any ship for the purpose of finding Sir John Franklin and his men.

Yours faithfully,
Mr. G. Shepherd
Engineer

EDITOR'S PAGE

In response to this newspaper's request for readers to suggest ways that Franklin and his men could be found, Mr. Jones of Whitby has sent in a sketch of a ship being lifted by three enormous hot air balloons attached to her upper deck.

23

Breaking through the ice

People did not realize the difficulties of searching in such extreme conditions. They did not know what a huge area Franklin was lost in. Britain, France, Holland, and Germany together would all fit into this area. It was a maze of islands and channels. Even where there was an open stretch of water, it was likely to freeze up behind a ship at any time, trapping it in.

An artist's impression of a sailing ship breaking through the huge sheets of ice.

Ice facts

The average thickness of ice in the Arctic seas is 6 to 9 feet, but it can be as much as 15 feet. That's even taller than two tall men standing on the shoulders of another.

Icebreakers

This is the Russian icebreaker *Yamal*.

We now know that the only way to break up and move through the Arctic ice would be by using a modern ship called an icebreaker.

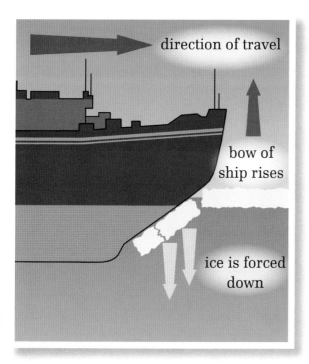

direction of travel

bow of ship rises

ice is forced down

An icebreaker does not smash *through* the ice. It has a specially shaped sloping **bow** that slides up on the ice, using the weight of the ship to break the chunks of ice beneath it. The wooden ships used by Franklin and the search parties were not big or powerful enough to do this. A modern icebreaker ship weighs nearly 14 times what Franklin's *Erebus* weighed!

News at last

Now . . . back to our search for Franklin. . . .

In 1859, fourteen years after Franklin set off, a message was found sealed in a tin and left in a cairn. The paper inside had two messages on it. They had been written within one and two years of the *Erebus* and *Terror* arriving in the region. The first described the island where Franklin and his man had spent the winter. It said, "All well." However, someone else had returned to the same spot a year later to add his own note—and by now the news was much worse. A number of men were dead, the ships had been abandoned, and the survivors were about to set off across the ice in search of safety. One of those who had died was Sir John Franklin.

The message left by Franklin's team.

Neither the writers of the messages nor any other of the 129 men on the expedition survived. Three graves, some bones, and many belongings were found scattered over a wide area. No one has ever been sure what went wrong —whether it was cold, starvation, **scurvy,** or some other illness, or a combination of several problems. Although they were trapped in the ice, it was felt that at least some of the men should have been able to make it to safety. Today, people still debate why no one survived.

Imagine how cold and lonely John Franklin and his men must have felt.

The Northwest Passage today

Sir John Franklin can be said to have "discovered" the Northwest Passage when you take into account all of his expeditions. However, the first person to actually sail through in one voyage was the Norwegian explorer Roald Amundsen in 1905.

Amundsen's ship the *Gjøa* was much smaller than the *Erebus* and *Terror* and was able to sail in places too shallow for Franklin's ships.

Norwegian explorer Roald Amundsen.

Scientists now tell us that the effects of global warming melting the Arctic ice might one day make the Northwest Passage relatively safe and easy to sail through. Despite this, the route through the Northwest Passage has still only been completed a few times. Some of those who claimed to have sailed the Passage were actually traveling in icebreakers. In 2000, a Canadian boat (the *St. Roch II*) sailed the Northwest Passage in nine weeks. The ice was not bad enough to stop it. Although this was unusual, it added to the fears about global warming. The ice is reported to be getting thinner, but it still takes an icebreaker ship to break through the ice where it exists.

Global warming and the Arctic

What is global warming?

Global warming (sometimes called the Greenhouse Effect) is the rise in the average temperature of Earth's atmosphere. Most scientists think that pollution from cars and airplanes is contributing to global warming.

Average temperatures in the Arctic are rising twice as fast as they are in the rest of the world.

Gases caused by pollution rise into the atmosphere and trap the sun's heat. This heat does not escape into space, so the planet gets warmer.

In recent times, the rise in temperature has caused more ice to melt than has happened for several centuries. Ice that had been around for 3,000 years started melting in the year 2000.

The end of the search?

In 2008, more than 160 years after Franklin set off on his final expedition, the Canadian government sent out the latest of many expeditions that have attempted to find the ships and perhaps discover what happened to their crews, but no further trace of the *Erebus* or *Terror* was found. Global warming, which is now melting the ice, may one day help to reveal the whereabouts of the ships, but for the time being, they lie waiting to be found—in the hidden depths.

> Global warming is a threat to the wildlife in the Arctic, such as polar bears.

> Did they ever find out what really happened to Franklin and his men?

> No, not yet, but people are still trying to find out!

Glossary

Arctic	the icy region around the most northern part, or top of Earth
Baffin Bay	a large body of sea off the coast of Greenland and opposite the entrance to the Northwest Passage
bow	the front end of a ship
cairn	a pile of stones left by explorers to show others where they have been, often marking a place where food and messages might be found
circumnavigate	to go all the way around
Inuit	the native people who live in the Arctic regions of northern Canada
knighted	to be given a title for outstanding achievement or service
moccasins	lightweight shoes traditionally used by various native peoples of North America
moss	a plain, green, grass-like plant
North Pole	the northernmost point of Earth
providence	what some people believe to be help from God or nature
scurvy	a disease caused by a lack of vitamin C (e.g., not having fresh fruit and vegetables to eat)
sonar	a system that uses sound to detect the location of objects

Index